The Path to GODLINESS
TITUS

by

Philip D. Jensen
&
Tony Payne

The Path to Godliness
© St Matthias Press, 1996

Published in the UK by
The Good Book Company
Elm House, 37 Elm Road
New Malden, Surrey KT3 3HB
Tel: 0845-225-0880
Fax: 0845-225-0990
e-mail: admin@thegoodbook.co.uk
website: www.thegoodbook.co.uk

Scripture taken from the HOLY BIBLE, NEW INTERNATIONAL VER-
SION. Copyright © 1973, 1978, 1984 International Bible Society. Used
by permission of Zondervan Publishers.

ISBN 1 875245 18 9

Typesetting and design by Matthias Media.
Cover illustration: Richard Knight
Printed in Hong Kong

Contents

How to make the most of these studies

1. What is an Interactive Bible Study?

These 'interactive' Bible studies are a bit like a guided tour of a famous city. The studies will take you through Paul's letter to Titus, pointing out things along the way, filling in background details, and suggesting avenues for further exploration. But there is also time for you to do some sight-seeing of your own—to wander off, have a good look for yourself, and form your own conclusions.

In other words, we have designed these studies to fall half-way between a sermon and a set of unadorned Bible study questions. We want to provide stimulation and input and point you in the right direction, while leaving you to do a lot of the exploration and discovery yourself.

We hope that these studies will stimulate lots of 'interaction'—interaction with the Bible, with the things we've written, with your own current thoughts and attitudes, with other people as you discuss them, and with God as you talk to him about it all.

2. The Format

Each study contains sections of text to introduce, summarize, suggest and provoke. We've left plenty of room in the margins for you to jot comments and questions as you read. Interspersed throughout the text are three types of 'interaction', each with their own symbol:

For starters
Questions to break the ice and get you thinking.

Investigate
Questions to help you investigate key parts of the Bible.

Think it Through

Questions to help you think through the implications of your discoveries and write down your own thoughts and reactions.

When you come to one of these symbols, you'll know that it's time to do some work of your own.

3. Suggestions for Individual Study

- Before you begin, pray that God would open your eyes to what he is saying in Titus and give you the spiritual strength to do something about it. You may be spurred to pray again at the end of the study.
- Work through the study, following the directions as you go. Write in the spaces provided.
- Resist the temptation to skip over the *Think it through* sections. It is important to think about the sections of text (rather than just accepting them as true) and to ponder the implications for your life. Writing these things down is a very valuable way to get your thoughts working.
- Take what opportunities you can to talk to others about what you've learnt.

4. Suggestions for Group Study

- Much of the above applies to group study as well. The studies are suitable for structured Bible study or cell groups, as well as for more informal pairs and threesomes. Get together with a friend/s and work through them at your own pace; use them as the basis for regular Bible study with your spouse. You don't need the formal structure of a 'group' to gain maximum benefit.
- It is *vital* that group members work through the study themselves *before* the group meets. The group discussion can take place comfortably in an hour (depending on how side-tracked you get!), but only if all the members have done the work and are familiar with the material.
- Spend most of the group time discussing the 'interactive' sections—*Investigate* and *Think it through*. Reading all the text together will take too long and should be unnecessary

if the group members have done their preparation. You may wish to underline and read aloud particular paragraphs or sections of text that you think are important.

- The role of the group leader is to direct the course of the discussion and to try to draw the threads together at the end. This will mean a little extra preparation—underlining important sections of text to emphasize, working out which questions are worth concentrating on, and being sure of the main thrust of the study. Leaders will also probably want to work out approximately how long they'd like to spend on each part.
- We haven't included an 'answer guide' to the questions in the studies. This is a deliberate move. We want to give you a guided tour of Titus not a lecture. There is more than enough in the text we have written and the questions we have asked to point you in what we think is the right direction. The rest is up to you.

For more input:
- See 'Tips for Leaders' on page 45.
- There is also a series of audio cassettes available which expound the relevant passages (see page 47 for details).

Before you begin

We recommend that before you start on Study 1, you take the time to read right through Titus in one sitting. This will give you a feel for the direction and purpose of the whole book and help you greatly in looking at each passage in its context.

1   A Helicopter *Joy-Ride*

Tucked down at the back of the New Testament, sandwiched between the well-known letters of Paul to Timothy and the equally well-known letter to the Hebrews, is Paul's short letter to his friend Titus. It is an obscure book to many 20th Century Christians, partly because we don't tend to study it very often, but also because we may be unsure how to apply such a personal and specific letter to our lives. Titus' circumstances were rather different from ours; the problems he faced and about which Paul wrote may seem foreign to us.

In another sense, however, Titus and his mates were not so different from us at all. They struggled with immorality and error among Christian leaders; they strived to live a consistently Christian life in a world hostile to the gospel; they needed encouraging about the basis and motivation of their lives as well as detailed teaching about behaviour. In other words, though their physical and cultural circumstances were quite different, their spiritual lives were very similar to our own.

The book of Titus lays before us a *path to godliness*. Though addressed to special circumstances, it gives us some general principles about what godliness is and how we can attain it. We need this teaching now as much as they did then.

Before we look at Paul's letter in detail, we need to take a helicopter ride over it. In this first study, we'll look at some of the surrounding territory (the background information), read Titus right through and get a feel for its contents and shape.

The story so far...

One good thing about the background to Titus is that it's easy to become an expert. There's not a lot to know. Titus (the man) is not mentioned in Acts, although his name pops up in Paul's other letters as a faithful and honest fellow-worker (e.g. 2 Cor 8:16-23; 12:18). We don't know very much about how Titus came to be in Crete, nor how the gospel came to Crete in the first place (Paul passed by the island on his way to Rome).

All the solid information we have about the circumstances on Crete and Paul's reasons for writing are contained in the letter itself, and that is where we now turn.

Investigate

Read the following questions and then read right through Titus, answering the questions as you go.

1. What do we learn about the character of the church in Crete:

the make up of the congregation?

the past history of the congregation?

the natural character of the Cretan people?

the way they became Christians?

the things that were threatening them?

2. What do you learn about Titus and his role in the church?

3. What do you learn about Paul and his reason for writing?

Passing the ball

In the great rugby game of life, the Saints are playing the Demons. One of the Saints' star players (Paul) is being tackled and like any good player, he stands in the tackle and looks to offload the ball. He knows that if the Saints are going to continue to go forward, he can't afford to go down with the ball. He has to pass it.

The urgent need for the ball to be passed is what lies behind Paul's letter to Titus (as well as his letters to Timothy). Paul is passionately concerned that the gospel be passed on to the next generation of Christians. People have been converted and churches have been planted, but if the work is to continue and grow, then the next generation of leaders must be equipped to take over. The future of Christianity is at stake.

More than this, Paul sees that the true gospel—the gospel which has been entrusted to him by God (1:3)—is continually under threat, both from a hostile world and from false teachers. As we will discover in our next study, the appointment and behaviour of godly elders (or overseers) is a key element in countering this threat.

To return to our rugby metaphor, we are at the end of a long back-line, and to reach us the ball has passed through quite a few pairs of hands (about 20 lifetimes separate us from Paul and Titus). However, it is the *same ball* and in Paul's letter to Titus we see it being passed for the first time. We see the gospel as it has been entrusted to Paul by God and the godly lifestyle that must accompany it. We see a fixed, given body of 'sound doctrine' which is only properly understood if it is lived.

Think it Through

1. What things bind us to the world of the first century? Based on your first reading of Titus, what things do we have in common with the Cretans?

2. From Titus, have a stab at defining what 'the ball' is that Paul is passing on (in a couple of sentences).

2 Teachers *True and False*

Leadership is a scandal in much of modern Christianity. In the face of an increasingly secular society, many Christian leaders seem either unsure of what their message should be, or incapable of living in accordance with it.

Leadership is an important subject in Paul's letter to Titus. As we look at the characteristics of elders and false teachers in chapter 1, we will discover significant implications not just for leaders, and for those who appoint leaders, but for the whole nature of Christianity.

An unfinished task

The place to begin our study of Titus is at 1:5 (we'll come back to 1:1-4). Here we have Paul's reason for leaving Titus in Crete in the first place, a summary of Titus' task and Paul's essential reason for writing:

> The reason I left you in Crete was that you might straighten out what was left unfinished and appoint elders in every town, as I directed you.

The work of the gospel in Crete needed straightening out and finishing. It was not only incomplete, it was also crooked, and Paul wanted this rectified as soon as possible.

This over-riding purpose permeates the rest of the letter. Titus was to appoint godly elders to shore up 'the common faith'; but he was also to take a personal role in getting the Cretan church back on the right track—by rebuking, teaching, encouraging, reminding and warning (1:13; 2:1,15; 3:1,10).

It is hard to read these words about 'appointing elders' without immediately thinking of our own church structures, with their elders, pastors, presbyters, bishops, priests, deacons or whatever. And certainly, Paul's words to Titus are very relevant to Christian leadership today. However, we must remember that what Paul meant by words like 'elder' or 'overseer' may be quite different from how we use the words. 'Elder' (v. 6) is a translation of the Greek word *presbuteros*, from which we also get the English words 'Presbyterian' and 'priest'. 'Overseer' (v. 7) is the Greek word *episcopos*, from which we get 'episcopal'. (Traditionally, *episcopos* has been translated as 'bishop'.)

In Paul's mind, there was no difference between an elder and an overseer; they were simply two different words to describe the same animal. (Note how he uses the two words interchangeably in vv. 6 and 7.) The way the words are used today, however, would suggest that there is a great deal of difference. In the 2000 years since Paul wrote these fairly simple words to Titus, volumes have been written, denominations have split and blood has been shed, all over theories of eldership, episcopacy and priesthood. By and large, these theories and the church structures they have spawned, are human in origin and bear all the marks of our human love of power.

For Paul and Titus, however, the theory and practice of elders/overseers was much more straightforward. In the face of opposition and threat, each congregation needed faithful and godly leaders who would stand firm against the opposition and encourage the church. This kind of function is conveyed in the very words 'elder' and 'overseer'. They were to be older, wiser, experienced Christians who were qualified to keep an eye on what was happening and act for the good of the congregation. This task is made explicit in v. 9:

> He [the elder/overseer] must hold firmly to the trust-worthy message as it has been taught, so that he can encourage others by sound doctrine and refute those who oppose it.

There was false teaching present in the Cretan churches and the elders were to play a key role in refuting it and encouraging the Christians to stick to the truth.

Read Titus 1:5-9.

1. What are marks of a true and godly teacher:

in behaviour?

in relation to doctrine?

Read Titus 1:10-16.

2. What are the general marks of a false teacher:

in behaviour?

in relation to doctrine?

3. What were the special characteristics of the Cretan false teachers?

Why does it matter?

You have no doubt picked up the strong contrast Paul draws between godly elders and false teachers, but you may ask: 'So what? What's all the fuss about? Aren't people allowed to express a different opinion without being silenced?'

If James Bond movies were still in fashion, a more politically correct version might be filmed and called *Live and Let Live*. Tolerance (or rather relativism) is one of the hallmarks of our modern Western society. In fact, if Paul was writing these words today, he would no doubt be labelled a 'fundamentalist' in the media. There might even be a campaign on behalf of the false teachers to gain them an equal say in how the church should be run.

Speculation aside, the apostle Paul obviously thought that the false teachers were a very serious problem. He denounces them in the strongest possible terms (see v. 16!). Why did it matter so much to Paul? Here are three reasons.

i. The consequences

The first and most obvious reason for Paul's concern was the havoc being wrought in the Cretan congregation. False teaching is rarely (if ever) an isolated, self-contained or purely intellectual phenomenon. Its consequences are almost always far-reaching and damaging to spiritual health. In this case, the urgent need to silence the false teachers is underscored by the consequences of their teaching—"they are ruining whole households by teaching things they ought not to teach" (1:11). This had to stop.

ii. The way to know God

However, there is a more profound reason why false teaching must be firmly dealt with, and it is a reason that Christians in the late twentieth century need to hear as much as anyone. In modern Western culture, most people believe that there are many ways to God. While Bible-believing Christians may be ready to proclaim that Christ is the unique and only way to God, this modern way of thinking (known as 'relativism') affects us more than we are aware. Whenever we are inclined to think that a particular brand of false teaching doesn't matter too much, or that mutually incompatible theologies can exist comfortably side-by-side in a congregation, then we betray how much we have been influenced by the mood of our day.

We cannot come to know the true and living God by intuition or by rational thought or by running an experiment or by seeing him on the back of our eyelids. The Bible is quite clear on this—we can only know anything about God because he *reveals* himself to us. He parts the curtain and brings up the lights. Our knowledge of God is not something we have attained through great effort or cleverness—it is entirely on God's initiative. We only know what he has chosen to tell us.

This way of thinking lies at the heart of the apostle Paul's life and thought. And it is also the basis for his very stern attitude towards the false teachers in Crete. It comes out in his opening greeting and description of himself. Let's take a look at it.

Investigate

Read Titus 1:1-4.

1. Paul sees his ministry as being for "the faith of God's elect and the knowledge of truth". What is the result (or accompaniment) of this faith and knowledge? Where does it lead to?

2. What is this faith and knowledge based on?

3. God has promised all this, but where do we hear this promise? How is it made known?

4. How does all this help explain Paul's attitude to the false teachers?

iii. The significance of teachers

If Christianity is based on a revealed message, sent from God, which promises eternal life and leads to a life of godliness, then we can see why true and godly teachers are so important.

Think about it for a minute. Our hope of eternal life is based on the promises of God—a set of promises that was revealed through the life and death of a first century Jew called Jesus and subsequently entrusted to his apostles. It is absolutely vital, therefore, that the promises of God are maintained from generation to generation. They must be defended and passed on faithfully, because our whole relationship with God (our faith and knowledge and godliness) are based on these promises. False teachers are *the* enemy because they destroy this true knowledge of God by distorting the given message. The true gospel must be safeguarded and used to encourage the brethren and refute error (Tit 1:9). We can begin to see why Paul was so concerned about the Cretan situation, and why the doctrinal maturity of the elders was so important.

If the gospel that has been entrusted to Paul leads to a life of godliness (v. 1), then we can also see why the *behaviour* of elders is so significant. Not only does it model the lifestyle which all Christians should pursue, but it demonstrates that the elders have truly understood the message that they are supposed to protect and proclaim. True knowledge of God leads to godliness; that is its very character. If we think we have grasped that knowledge and yet there is no godliness in our lives, then we are self-deluded—we have not grasped the message at all, and we are certainly in no position to teach and lead others.

The ungodly behaviour of the false teachers damns their teaching, for behaviour and doctrine are inextricably bound together. Bad behaviour reveals an underlying ignorance of God; and bad behaviour also distorts the message, as we seek to rationalize and justify our lifestyle.

As Paul looked to the future, he saw the fundamental importance of sound doctrine and godly living for the survival of the young churches under his care. We neglect this twofold emphasis to our peril.

Think it through

1. Why is it important that we know our teachers and can see their lives?

2. In appointing leaders (whether for congregations, youth groups, beach missions or Sunday School classes), what personal qualities should we look for?

3. What characteristics do we often look for instead?

4. Although this passage speaks directly about elders (true and false), what does it tell us about the lives of all Christians?

5. What does this passage stir us to pray for?

Quiet Time - Session 2

3 Motivation for a *Changed Lifestyle*

Being a Christian must affect the way we live. We sense that this is so, almost instinctively, and we cringe when Christians (especially those in the public eye) act as if this is not the case. The Christian hypocrite, whose mouth says one thing but whose life says another, is an object of derision.

Even so, working out just how our knowledge should affect our behaviour can be confusing. There are times when 'Christian' behaviour seems indistinguishable from 'non-Christian' behaviour (both would agree, for example, that stealing is wrong); and there are other times where we are at odds with our non-Christian neighbours (e.g. over sexual morality). And when Christians fail to live by their profession, or seriously water it down, it muddies the waters still further.

The apostle Paul was convinced that knowledge of God should lead to godliness (Tit 1:1-2). In fact, this was one of his primary concerns about the church in Crete. The Cretan national character did not provide the best pattern of life to have been raised in and the Cretan Christians (under Titus) needed to grow and develop into changed people; people who were to "devote themselves to doing what is good" (cf. Tit 1:12-13; 3:14).

However, we need to be aware of two possible problems as we approach this whole subject: legalism and licence.

Problems
i. Legalism
Legalism takes several forms, but the most common in our society is the widespread perception that 'being good' equals 'being Christian'. This is perhaps the single greatest misunder-

---

* Keen observers may notice something odd as we proceed through this study—we have missed out Titus 2:1-10. This has been a deliberate move. We thought it better to look at the *motivation* for a godly lifestyle (in Tit 2:11-14 and 3:1-8) before filling out the *content* of a godly lifestyle (in Tit 2:1-10 and 3:9f.). Stay tuned.

---

standing of Christianity in our community. Many people believe that Christianity is all about, or mainly about, morality; that it's about what you *do*. The activities of some Christians unfortunately do little to dispel this misconception.

A more 'religious' version of legalism tries to *add* things to our basic trust in Jesus. In Paul's day, he was confronted by a circumcision club who thought that it was necessary for all Christians to rigorously obey the Jewish law as well as put their faith in Christ for forgiveness. In our day, we see this among some sub-Christian sects who require certain patterns of obedience in order to earn salvation. And we see it among some mainline Christian groups when they insist that certain practices done certain ways (e.g. baptism, the Lord's Supper) are *essential* for our salvation.

Legalism is disastrous, because it attacks the cross of Christ. Paul wanted the Cretans to lead a changed lifestyle but he didn't want to lay a new law on them. He didn't want to say to them, "You need to do this and this and this in order to be saved".

ii. Licence

The second, and opposite, problem is licence. This is the view that since we are completely forgiven through Christ's death, how we live doesn't really matter. If there are no laws hanging over our heads, then we are free to do as we please. We are free to indulge ourselves, because we can always go back to God for forgiveness if the need arises.

Paul was not too impressed with this 'blank cheque' style of Christianity. He didn't want legalism, with its carrot-and-stick approach to life, but neither did he want the Cretan Christians to think that they could simply live as they pleased. Paul knew that it *mattered* how you lived, but he had a problem: how do you move a donkey without a carrot or stick?

The answer is in Titus 2:11-14, which we will now look at in some detail.

Investigate

Read Titus 2:1-14.

1. The word 'for' links vv. 11-14 with the verses before it. What do you think is the significance of this word?

2. The word 'grace' is well-known in our culture as a religious word. It has many meanings, ranging from an incantation said before meals to a way to address holy persons ('your grace'). Here in Titus it carries its usual biblical meaning, which is something like 'generosity'. Grace is undeserved, unmerited favour, in this case from God. See if you can think up an illustration or an event from your life that illustrates the concept of grace.

The grace of God is said to do two things in this passage: it brings salvation to all men (v. 11) and it teaches or instructs us (v. 12). Let's look at each of these in turn.

Grace that saves

3. 'Salvation' is another religious word. It simply means 'rescue'. It is perhaps stating the obvious, but before someone can be rescued, they need to be in some sort of danger or trouble. Is there any indication in vv. 11-14 about what it is we've been rescued from?

4. According to Titus 2:11, the grace of God has appeared to 'all men'. This could conceivably mean:
   a) all male persons;
   b) the whole of mankind;
   c) all kinds of people.
Given the context of this verse (coming straight after vv. 1-10), which of these three options do you think Paul meant?

5. Looking through the rest of our passage (vv. 11-14), what 'appearing' do you think Paul is referring to? Give reasons for your answer.

6. How did this salvation take place? How was it done? (Try to put it in your own words without any jargon.)

7. What was the underlying purpose for the rescue?

8. What are the implications of this understanding of salvation for:

the legalism problem

the licence problem

Grace that trains

9. The grace of God that has appeared is also said to go on teaching or training us. It doesn't just save us once off and then we carry on with life as before. It trains us to live differently. *How* do you think this might happen?

10. What two things will it train us to do? Expand on what you think each of these things mean.

11. How does this new way of living affect our relationship with:

ourselves

other people

God

The path to godliness

In our last study (about teachers true and false), we saw that there is a close connection between *knowledge* and *behaviour*. The true message from God leads to godliness, and we can recognize false gospels because they do not yield a godly lifestyle. That connection is reinforced in Titus 2:11-14.

The grace of God that has saved us through the death of Jesus also trains us in how we should live. If we have received this generosity from God—if it has released us from slavery and purified us to be worthy of belonging to God—then our lives will be different. As we wait for Jesus to return (v. 13) and as we call to mind all that he has done for us, we are motivated to say 'no' and 'yes'—no to all that drags us back to our former slavery; and yes to the way of life that we were always meant to live, the way of life that puts us both in control of ourselves, and in right relation to others and God.

When we are caught in a current about 100m off the beach and the lifesaver appears and drags us onto his surfboard, what happens next? We don't ask to be thrown back in; nor do we expect to spend the rest of our lives on the board. We head for the beach to begin a new life, a life in which we might be more careful about where and how we swim. Our salvation is not an end in itself. It is but the first stage in a whole new life, a life lived for God rather than for ourselves.

Think it Through

1. Do you know this grace of God we have been talking about? If so, how has it changed the way you live?

2. Our motives are often hard to untangle, and we should not expect to achieve complete purity of motive until heaven. Given this, what different motives do you think lie behind the way you live at the moment?

3. Which of these should you try to change?

4 Why *Born Again* Christianity is *Authentic*

When was the last time you described yourself as a 'born again Christian'?

I'm willing to bet that you can't remember, either because it was about 20 years ago or because the words have never passed your lips. It's not a title we like to go by these days. It conjures up images of tub-thumping evangelists with lots of teeth (and lots of money). It's a plastic, phoney kind of expression in our society, always to be pronounced with a slight American accent ('Ahm borrn agin').

There are no doubt many reasons why people don't like born again Christianity, but it is curious that many Christians also find the term just a little objectionable. It is, after all, a very biblical way of speaking (Jesus was not embarrassed to use it in John 3). What is it about 'born again' that we don't like? Here are four suggestions.

i. It's hypocritical

We have seen too many religious phoneys who go by the name 'born again' to be very fond of the words. American politicians, it seems, adopt the 'born again' tag to secure the Christian vote (which, in America, is substantial). They start attending church and going to prayer breakfasts just in time for the presidential race to start.

This is perhaps a particularly American phenomenon, but it prejudices our attitude to being 'born again'.

ii. It's threatening

Many people prefer Christianity to look like Doris Day did in some of her movies—shot with a soft lens so that the edges are blurred. This sort of 'blurred again' Christianity is much easier to cope with than the rather abrupt, absolutist born again variety. It's more comfortable, especially for fence-sitters.

To claim to be born again is to make a fairly stark and

threatening sort of claim. It implies that you have made a whole new start, that you are the genuine article. It exudes an air of confident self-identity. It says, "I am in and you are out".

This threatens people, both Christians and non-Christians. The non-Christian feels alienated, and finds such a sharp, picket fence difficult to sit on. But Christians, too, can feel uneasy about the whole subject—how can I be sure that I am one of the true Christians and not a counterfeit?

iii. It's arrogant

Being born again also seems to imply a degree of arrogance. If I label myself 'born again' then it seems that I'm claiming to be better than you. Born again Christianity conveys a holier-than-thou sort of impression.

This is especially so for the many people in our society who equate being Christian with *being good*. If Christianity is all about morality, then surely the genuine, true-blue, born again Christian is claiming to be especially good. And because we suspect that they aren't that good, we label them an arrogant hypocrite.

iv. It's immoral

Others complain that being born again seems like a licence to do whatever you like (see our comments on "licence' in Study 3). If being a Christian means starting from scratch and having everything forgiven (being born again), then what motive is there for morality? It's not only unjust that immoral people should be given a clean slate like that, but it discourages others from doing their best. Or so it is argued.

Why born again Christianity is authentic

Despite these objections, we need to come to terms with the fact that being born again is an authentic, biblical way to describe what it means to be a Christian. It is historically authentic, in that the term is found in the original documents of the New Testament on the lips of Jesus, Peter, Paul and James. But it is also theologically authentic (as we shall see) because it describes something of the essential nature of becoming (and being) a Christian. Jesus went so far as to say that "no-one can see the kingdom of God unless he is born again" (Jn 3:3).

Let's look at our passage and see what it tells us.

Investigate

Read Titus 3:1-8.

1. In order to gain a feel for how this short section flows, fill in the following summary of verses 3-8. (Complete each phrase from the passage and briefly explain it in your own words.)

We were once...

But God...

not because...

but because...

through...

so that...

2. Verse 2 talks about showing "true humility to all men". How do you think this relates to the verses that follow?

3. How should the massive change or new start that is described in this passage affect the way we live?

Paul's dazzling description of born again Christianity turns many of our perceptions upside down. According to Paul, being born again or 'reborn' is not an arrogant proclamation of how good we are, but a stunning admission of how enslaved and foolish we once were and how miraculously and undeservingly we have been changed. God has scrubbed us clean, drenching us with his Spirit, to make us worthy heirs of his kingdom.

However, at least one of the charges people bring against born again Christianity is true: it is threatening. If becoming an heir of eternal life is only achieved through this radical transformation of 'rebirth and renewal', then we start to do something that other people hate. We start to draw lines. We say, in effect, that those who have not tasted this saving act of God, are foolish, deceived and enslaved, as we once were (v. 3). This will not win us friends. As Paul says elsewhere, those who are outside of Christ find the gospel a terrible stench to their nostrils. Those who are being saved find it the sweetest of all smells (2 Cor 2:14-16).

There is only one brand of Christianity, the original and the best. New Testament Christianity is about a total transformation of sinful people through the merciful power of God. That's born again Christianity, and it's the real thing.

Think it through

1. How might this understanding of the Christian life affect our prayers? What would it lead us to pray for?

2. Why do some people find the message of God's grace offensive? What is it about the message that gets under our skin?

3. Why should being born again make you truly humble rather than arrogant?

4. Would you say that your own life is marked by true humility to all?

5. Why should being 'reborn' minimize hypocrisy rather than promote it?

6. Why should being 'reborn' lead to morality rather than immorality?

5
The Content of
a *Changed* Lifestyle

With the sort of painful clarity that only advertising can achieve, the billboard said it all: "This month in [Magazine X], the complete guide to success in career, health, sex, finance, beauty, travel and much, much more".

We can only wonder what the "much, much more" included. Certainly, it is hard to think of a more apt summary of all that our society wants. The twentieth century person is into 'lifestyle'. We don't just want to exist—to be born, consume and die—we want the 'good life' (whatever it is). Our whole social structure is based on this constant desire for a higher or better standard of living. Governments rise and fall on their ability to deliver it; we work all our lives in order to attain it (if not for ourselves, then at least 'for the kids'); and businessmen and advertisers grow fat by persuading us that their particular products are an essential part of attaining that 'lifestyle'.

This desirable lifestyle is defined for us in all kinds of ways. We watch our parents and learn what is worth (or not worth) striving for. We absorb values in the classroom, in the workplace, at the pub, and especially in the blue light of our TV screens.

Christianity is also about a lifestyle, one which has its own particular content and motivations, and which often stands quite opposed to what the rest of our society thinks of as the good life. In our last two studies, we looked at the motivation for a Christian lifestyle. In this and the following study, we'll start to fill out the content of Christian living, as we find it in Paul's letter to Titus. To put it another way, we have looked at the start of the path to godliness, and the forces that keep us moving forward; now we'll look at the content of godliness that we're striving for.

Investigate

1. Look back over Studies 3 and 4. Summarize the motives that lie behind a Christian lifestyle.

Read Titus 2:1-10.

2. What other motivations can you find in Titus 2:1-10? Can you see any connections between knowledge/doctrine and godliness?

3. In Titus 2:1-10, Paul follows a favourite first century practice of describing the way people should live in terms of a 'household code' (for other New Testament examples see Eph 5; Col 3; 1 Pet 2:13-3:7). He works through the key social relationships and describes the appropriate Christian behaviour for each group.

Write down the things Paul directs Titus to teach each group and note any areas that you don't understand.

Older men

Older women

Younger women

Younger men

Slaves

The perverse unpopularity of the Christian

As we work through God's guidelines for a 'good' lifestyle, we're
struck by how appealing and yet how unpopular these values
are. In many respects, our non-Christian society is strangely
attracted to these values. Who would not want older men to be
temperate and dignified, worthy of respect and showing wis-
dom and love? Who could not but be drawn to the idea of a
devoted, pure young woman who has been taught to love her
husband and children by an older, wiser woman? Who would
not want workers to be respectful, hard-working and trustwor-
thy? Or a self-controlled, upright young man?

Our society longs for a set of values like this and yet, perversely, when confronted with them, refuses to live this way. And when Christians try to live this way, we are ridiculed. We find ourselves in conflict with our workmates when we choose to act honestly when they are all abusing the system. We are often scorned by our peers when we choose purity over decadence, and uprightness over shame. We are pressured on all sides to go with the flow, to adopt the same materialistic, selfish lifestyle as our neighbours, to sacrifice our family lives to the gods of achievement, money and job satisfaction.

Paul's 'household code' proposes a radical alternative lifestyle, motivated by the grace of God in Christ and defined by what pleases God. Making this lifestyle our own will draw us into conflict with our non-Christian world at various points and we need to be ready for it. But if God's grace has entered our lives, it will keep teaching and urging us to face that conflict, to say no and to say yes.

Think it through

1. Which of the groups do you fit into? What is God telling you to do here? (Be specific and practical.)

2. Perhaps the most controversial of Paul's directions concerns young women. To suggest that young women should be 'busy at home' and 'be subject to their husbands' is hardly popular in our society. It is in areas like these that we find the clash of values most severe.

Do these verses forbid a woman from working in a job outside the home?

What principles or values about family life are being taught here?

From verses 3-5, would you say that loving your husband/children comes easily and naturally?

3. 'Self-control' features prominently in this passage (in fact for young men, it is a blanket statement that seems to cover everything). What does our society think about self-control? In what areas do you find self-control difficult? (Be honest.)

4. How might these values affect your godliness:

at work

with your family

at church

6

The Path to *Godliness*

In our last study, we began to look at the content of a Christian lifestyle in Titus 2:1-10. We saw that Paul wanted Titus to instruct the people to live godly lives in accordance "with sound doctrine" (Tit 2:1). In this study we'll continue to think about that content by looking further at chapter 3. This is fairly straightforward material, but it requires us to think seriously about our lives.

At the end of this study, we'll also look back over all that we've done and try to solidify it in our minds.

Investigate

In Titus 2:1-10, we saw Paul's 'household code' for the different social groupings in the Cretan church. In chapter 3, he talks about their behaviour as citizens and as members of the congregation.

Read Titus 3:1-3.

1. As the Cretan Christians relate to the world around them, what is to mark their behaviour?

2. How does this behaviour contrast with what they were once like (and presumably what their neighbours are still like)?

Read Titus 3:4-14.

3. In their relationships with each other as a church, what should the Cretan Christians avoid. Why?

4. What should they pursue? Why?

Think it through

1. As we relate to our world, what things make it difficult for us to be subject to authorities, to be peaceable and gentle?

2. What implications do these verses have for Christian social or political activism?

3. Why do we find controversy and argument so attractive?

4. What issues today might fall into the 'profitless controversy' category?

5. What does v. 14 teach us about the godly attitude to work?

The path to godliness

Paul's short letter to Titus, even though written in a time and place far removed from our own, teaches us important things about living as Christians. It teaches us that Christianity is not simply a body of doctrine, nor merely a code of morality. It is a relationship with God, initiated and established by God, based on a true knowledge of him, a knowledge which leads to a radically changed life.

This is the path to godliness. It is a simple path, yet a narrow one, for it avoids the errors that are so prevalent in our time. It does not diminish the crucial importance of sound doctrine (as so many do today), and neither does it drive a wedge between what we know and how we live (as many others also do). It keeps the two bonded tight together. True knowledge of God is the basis for godliness. If we do not have godliness, then we have not understood the knowledge of God; and conversely, if we don't know the truth about God, we have no hope of pleasing him and participating in the eternal life he has promised.

We've looked at these things (and more) over the last several weeks and now is the time to try to pull it all together. Look back briefly at the material we have covered. Then close your notes (and your Bible) and see if you can answer the following questions. They are not a 'test'—there are no marks or certificates. These summary questions are designed to help you revise what Titus is about and to entrench it in your mind.

1. Where was Titus?

2. What had Paul left Titus to do?

3. What two words describe the leadership ministry to which Titus was to appoint people?

4. What were the sorts of characteristics that Titus was to look for in suitable people for this ministry?

6. Why is it so important for teachers to display godliness in their lives?

7. What is the result of true Christian knowledge?

8. What is the motivation for a changed lifestyle?

9. What is 'grace'?

10. What two things does 'grace' do?

11. In Titus 3:5, we are told that God saved us:

    not because…

    but because…

12. What will be our attitude to others (i.e. other sinners) if we have been reborn through God's mercy?

13. How do Christians receive the Holy Spirit?

14. Summarize the Christian lifestyle of:

    the older man

the older woman

the younger woman

the younger man

the slave

15. Summarize how we Christians should relate to the non-Christian world?

Tips for *leaders*

Studying Titus

The studies in *The Path to Godliness*, like all of the Interactive and Topical Bible Studies from Matthias Media, are aimed to fall somewhere between a sermon and a set of unadorned discussion questions. The idea is to provide a little more direction and information than you would normally see in a set of printed Bible studies, but to maintain an emphasis on personal investigation, thought, discovery and application. We aim to give input and help, without doing all the work for the student.

Like all our studies, these are designed to work in a group on the assumption that the group members have worked through the material in advance. If this is not happening in your group it will obviously change the way you lead the study.

If the group is preparing...

If all is well, and the group is well-prepared, then reading through *all* the text, and answering *all* the questions will be time consuming and probably quite boring. It is not designed to work this way in a group.

The leader needs to go through the study thoroughly in advance and work out how to lead a group discussion using the text and questions as a *basis*. You should be able to follow the order of the study through pretty much as it is written. But you will need to work out which things you are going to omit, which you are going to glide over quite quickly, and which you are going to concentrate on and perhaps add supplementary discussion questions to.

Obviously, as with all studies, this process of selection and augmentation will be based on what your *aims* are for this study for your particular group. You need to work out where you want to get to as a main emphasis or teaching point or application point at the end. The material itself will certainly head you in a particular direction, but there will usually be various emphases you can bring out, and a variety of applications to think about.

The slabs of text need to be treated as a resource for discussion, not something to be simply read out. This will mean highlighting portions to talk about, adding supplementary discussion questions and ideas to provoke discussion where you think that would be helpful for your particular group, and so on.

The same is true for the *Investigate* and *Think it through* questions. You need to be selective, according to where you want the whole thing to go. Some questions you will want to do fairly quickly or omit altogether. Others you will want to concentrate on—because they are difficult or because they are crucial or both—and in these cases you may want to add a few questions of your own if you think it would help.

You may also need to add some probing questions of your own if your group is giving too many 'pat' answers, or just reproducing the ideas in the text sections without actually grappling with the biblical text for themselves.

There is room for flexibility. Some groups, for example, read the text and do the *Investigate* questions in advance, but save the *Think it through* questions for the group discussion.

If the group isn't preparing...

This obviously makes the whole thing a lot harder (as with any study). Most of the above still applies. But if your group is not doing much preparation, your role is even more crucial and active. You will have to be even more careful in your selection and emphasis and supplementary questions—you will have to convey the basic content, as well as develop it in the direction of personal application. Reading through the *whole* study in the group will still be hard going. In your selection, you will probably need to read more sections of text together (selecting the important bits), and will not be able to glide over comprehension questions so easily.

If the group is not preparing, it does make it harder—not impossible, but a good reason for encouraging your group to do at least some preparation.

Conclusion

No set of printed studies can guarantee a good group learning experience. No book can take the place of a well-prepared thoughtful leader who knows where he or she wants to take the group, and guides them gently along that path.

Our Bible studies aim to be a resource and handbook for that process. They will do a lot of the work for you. All the same, they need to be *used* not simply followed.